A
Rose

Blooms
In Winter

Khalil Ali

First Printing: © 2013 by Khalil Ali
Cover illustration by Queen LaZae Ali

ISBN 13: 978-0-692-66251-9

For more information regarding personal appearances, interviews or purchases please contact the publisher at:

King and Queen Publishing
Kingandqueenpublish.com
contact@kingandqueenpublish.com

Acknowledgements

I would like to begin this book as I begin every great endeavor; with the blessing and favor of the Almighty Creator of all the systems of knowledge, All the Worlds and of the entire Universe, Allah (which means in Arabic- The God). I hope everyone that has decided to take the time to read these thoughts and emotions of mine that you find great pleasure in them and that perhaps you not only obtain a glimpse into my inner being but that perchance I am able to help you to see your own as well. I would like to say thank you to my beloved, beautiful, tenacious and ornery wife, Renae, thank you for pressing me to do something with these thoughts and even though you seem to enjoy stressing me out and pick at me about nothing; I love you just the same and more each day. Thank you to all of my rambunctious children, D'Ronta, Laxaviera, Miranda, Ke'Von, Nehemiah and Amyrah, you all have indeed shown me the joy and pain of parenthood...you may not understand it all now but believe me in time indeed you shall. I would like to also give a special thank you to my loving, patient and caring mother, Mary; without you momma I don't think that I would have been able to get to the point of trying to want to do better in life. You have been the instrument of Almighty God that was to help me reach the path towards all that is good, wholesome and right. I love you and thank you more than words could ever begin to express. I also thank my dad,

Charles, for being as hard on me as you were and still are. It's because of that pressure that the lump of coal is becoming a diamond and that I have been more equipped to conquer obstacles that venture onto my path. I also thank my entire family, especially my Aunt Jeannette and Uncle Johnny for allowing me to stay with you all during my transition as well as the laundry, food and support- thank you so very much. To all of my brothers and sisters in my Little Rock, AR Islamic community (Islamic Center for Human Excellence) I thank you so very much for the opportunities that you gave me, words of encouragement, enlightenment and just know that we shall continue to work together to accomplish all that has been started. To all of my brothers and sisters behind those walls of correction I say to you- never give up or give in, unless you are giving yourself up to The God and getting involved in all that He has directed you to do to uplift others more so than yourself. These pages are my thoughts laid out before you; it was this that helped me to not only find peace in the midst of confusion but also to find the part of me that I didn't know was there.

Preface

A Rose Blooms in Winter: *Life Liberty & the Pursuit of Happiness*, is a composition of moments in time that reflect not only the thoughts and transformation of the author but also of the environment surrounding him. This is to serve as a symbol of love and devotion to the uplifting and improvement of all the black/African-Americans/people of color/ global majority and not as a tool of hate for anyone. The black Rose is symbolic of something that is beautiful yet often overlooked and underappreciated. It is given the imagery of being associated with death, Goth and all sorts of negative connotations; however, they are quite rare and stunning in their very nature. It takes time, patience and skill to grow such a rose and even then it may or may not develop into a pure black beauty; the author is such a rose. He is a black man that is continually blooming in the cold frost of winter and snow (i.e. living in a white society). Society, "in America we have been culturally conditioned to believe that black is inferior, white is superior and the manifestation of that is that African Americans are undervalued, underestimated and marginalized"- Joe Madison; yet they continue to bloom and develop into a beautiful black roses. The subtitle is also symbolic of a few things. The first being the obvious- the US Constitution and what it said is to be available for all persons that reside within the confines of the very nature of its construction. Life is the source of creation and the desire of every person that exists- love. Regardless of the individual, we all have a portion of our being that not only wants it but also wishes to give it. Liberty is as it denotes; citizens of any society not only request it but in far too many instances must continually demand respect and justice. To be treated with respect is not only a right but also a requirement for proper balance in an actual civilization. After one has begun the process of seeking life and liberty; they will find themselves fulfilling the last portion of the statement and constantly being in pursuit of maintaining it. Neither love nor liberty come freely, as we have seen, they both come at a cost; that may have paid for with the ultimate price- their very lives. This has been the case for centuries prior to now and unfortunately perhaps for many centuries to come. As long as there exist a cast system in which there are the have and have nots, a 1% that has 99% of the wealth and the 99% barely holding on to the 1% of the remaining. The 1% shall always have to struggle to have what all men & women should naturally have- respect. Respect in the sense that there shouldn't be an invisible line between those that have and those that have not. Especially when the global majority (black and brown faces) are forced into remaining in the position of the have not's. Hopefully, this book will serve as a catalyst to expedite the process of Lazarus coming back to life after being asleep for far too long...... Lazarus come forth!

Contents of Liberty

Contents of Life

Liberty

10th Power

Now if Oprah is the voice of 10 to the 10th Power, then who is one of less nobility? Perhaps it's not about who says it just as long as it gets said. So what if I were to voice myself or rather be the voice of 10 to the 10th Power; maybe no one would even take the time to listen, maybe they would? Regardless of which shouldn't the words still be said. With each word must be truth and power. Each syllable should be for a cause and not just because. They should be for every child that cries themselves to sleep. For every mother that has endured being beat to a state of temporary death only to wake up to the funeral or her child. For every father that has lost his children just because someone decided they wanted personal gain through pointless wars. For every sister and brother herded and treated worse than cattle. For every Native labeled as a "barbaric Indian". All the Latinos paid less and treated worse simply due to the fact they refuse to leave behind their culture. For all Asians, Arabs, and the Afro-centric labeled as gooks, terrorist and niggers. We must rise above these forms of diversity from adversity. Each one of us must be 10 to the 10th Power and be united as the strong fist that is held high in the air.

Abandoned Child

Is my heart truly beating or is it just my imagination?
Am I actually living this life or am I in a state of deep
contemplation?
Who am I to deny myself for a cause I do not believe in?
Or even to object to the realness of my undefined kin
Must my mind continue to wonder and probe the space between
then and now?
Please motion to the valet to bring my subconscious around
I seem to have left my conscious at home and I'll be damned if
I walk
Opportunity runs every 15 minutes and I'm blessed with the
ability to talk
Get your mind right Pharaoh and let my people go
Through each century the slave mentality is all they seem to
know
We weren't created like this, we were made like this, by those
that kill our pride
We would know them all but we live with our eyes openly
closed wide
Our lives are full of deception fueled by lies that we have
grown to believe
Although the child was killed at birth it soon began to grow like
a weave
So it was denied for some time in fact to some it shall always
be
Abandoned yet never forgotten from now till eternity.

America

What's wrong, as a matter of a fact what's really going on?
Why the need for a battle with someone else when the war is
inside of your own?
You say that your actions are justified by history and future
actions
When truthfully it's your ego and personal ass-sumptions that
has killed my sons
My daughters you have raped and beaten for so long they no
longer know themselves
My children are believing that they should seek out temporary
superficial wealth
They once passed creativity amongst one another out on the
corner of the blocks
Now they pass around 40's, blunts and bullets inside plastic
glocks
Our neighborhoods are filled with ideas and notions that were
injected into us
Product from overseas infiltrated our families and make believe
fantasies of a man named Isha
Stop thinking that life is a cat walk and you can walk on
everyone that's not of you
You will have to atone for the wrongs and heartaches you have
put people through
Why do you believe that the rules and laws do not apply to
you?
When will you learn that hell's flame will be fueled by the
things you do
Now is the time you should begin to turn from your wicked
ways and begin anew
Change the condition within yourself so that the condition will
change what you have been allowed to do.

Beware

Now a days my words are all I seem to own
In a world filled with chaos they make me a King on a
throne
Or perhaps they help me escape a world I wish to forget
A world without love I can't seem to fathom it
Which is odd because a world with it I can't receive
Who's to blame that what created us we can no longer
conceive
Creation begins on the inside then moves outward
As well as death when it is as two faced as a sword
Don't worry be happy was a #1 hit
Now a days to be happy is to see someone else worrying
over some unnecessary shit
Whatever happened to karma and quoting "peace not war"?
Who am I kidding just-US and 3K slapping that notion
right on the floor?
So where is this so called devil in disguise?
Just look for the "Honest John smile" and stereotypical
good eyes
The thief could be the hue of the true that's betwixt the air
Or perhaps just the curvaceous silhouette of buyer beware.

Black Stuff

"Are you down with that Black Stuff"?
Why wouldn't I be, I could never be black enough
I love to stay out in the sun and not burn
To walk down the street to only have your head turn
To be the envy of every culture
To have you and your friends prey on me like a vulture
My people are beautiful and the maker of all
Even the shortest of us stand 10 feet tall
Who else can say they come from the original Kings and
Queens?
Who do you think thought up and invented damn near
everything?
From the words you use to the things you wear
From the religion you believe down to even how you wear
your hair
Who else can survive anything and still manage a smile?
How many do you know can be so determined to walk for
miles and miles?
Look throughout time and I'm sure you'll find millions of
black faces
Some you would have never known in some of the most
exquisite places

In Egypt, Babylon and Timbuktu
Over to the Caribbean, Americas and next door to you
Yes I love "That Black Stuff" with all my might
From the fat lips, nose and booty to the hair nappy and dark as night
We are so black and beautiful that it should be a crime
In fact that is why we get harassed all the time
People are so jealous of what and who they can't be
It's not my fault you're weak, feeble, twisted and demented
Somethings will and will never be, that's just the way the Lord intended
Black people embrace our culture, race and our past
Some things were stolen from us but some things will always last.

Black Stuff II

Black Man, Black Prince, Black King
Black god, Black Throne, Black Being
Black Woman, Black goddess, Black Queen
My comfort, my treasure, my everything
Black House, Black Land, Black owned
This life of mine is more than gold
The truth was embedded and never sold
Black children are crying day and night
Nightmare of Black in white light
Born, live and die in this skin of Black
Some love while the rest just loath it
Never fake it, just make it and die for this shit
Black Genius, Black Minds and Black I chose
Black pimp that real and fuck them pale ho's
Black people in 4 shades with minds in stages of 3
A circumference of 9 keeps us in completely unity
Black Mother, Black Father, Black Love, Black Soul
Black People unite and complete the Black Goal
Black dance, Black movement, Black Strength, Black
Finesse
Black Sister, Black Brother celebrate your True Blackness.

Crystal Clear

Why question that which you know to be true

Keep it simple people, keep it you

Why change what's real into something make believe?

When reality is crystal clear quit obscuring what's easy to

perceive.

Nutty Squirrel

It only takes a second for me to be knocked off my rocka
Brain thoughts stinking like they need some Binaca
Personality becomes spilt like a Gemini from waves that
are wicked
It's good against evil so I guess that makes me conflicted
A simple lack of information causes the deepest cut
Regardless the outcome, just give this squirrel a nut
Pure truth without holding anything back
To Hell with what you don't wanna hear, now how you
love that!

Cramped Spaces

What happens when you become surrounded by voided brains?
Will you begin to live and think the same?
Does your perception of reality become disturbed or perplexed?
What's to happen with the rest of you, will it die off next
Sometimes I want to just scream, "My God why have you forsaken me!"
However, I soon realized that that could never be
Maybe one day all my questions and the world mysteries will be answered
Because giving in to ignorance isn't an option, that's for damn sure
My only words at times are Aoodu Billihi Minash Shatan-ir Rajeem
Imagine that, me seeking refuge from that which is within me
Me fighting a battle against the other version of me
The sane and perfected being vs. the instable and devious one
So in the end I still lose, only the amount depends on the exact outcome.

Caged Beast

Loosen my shackles and watch me roam

Refuse me my rights, you could never go home

Since they say I'm a menace I must be confined

Sex on the beach- not while I'm doing 70% of my time

Just give me 5 walk me downs while I walk down this bid

Maintain my pride but how could you have done what you

did

Although you may shackle my hands and feet together

My mind and spirit is one battle you will lose forever

Keep your distance from me; after all I am a caged beast

Verbally slice you open and on your soul I shall feast

I'm a beast y'all, a beast on the prowl

I'm a beast y'all, a beast don't you hear my growl

Break loose from these shackles yes the time is near

The countdown has begun and detonation is what you fear.

Caged Bird

What makes the caged bird sing?

With a heart of sorrow and a voice never trembling

Strong and proud although behind the smile lies tears

Carrying a heavy burden for so many years

A song of triumph over persecution and never defeat

Stride through beatings like a fast drum beat

Eyes as fierce as an eagle looking for its prey

Although the 12 feet cage shrinks 10 feet each day

The caged bird continues to just sing and sing

Looking for hope when none ever seems to be lurking

---Yet still he sings—

So sing little one sing your heart out

Sing for freedom, justice and Equality throughout

Sing for all to hear and see

Sing the song that weighs on your heavy heart

Sing until the chains and bars come bursting apart!

Self -Consciousness

Sometimes in life we experience situations in which we may begin to question why certain things (bad events) happened. During those moments in our lives we must realize that it was for a reason that sometimes we may not become aware of until later. However it would still behoove us to understand the amount of strength, power and knowledge we have just acquired. It has yet to become wisdom because we have yet to understand it but once we do we will be able to truly mature as it was planned prior to the moment of enlightenment. We love ourselves so that we will know how to love others, be loved, and not be loved. Even in the most heart stricken and down trodden of times we must continue to strive for greatness. Each day that we are blessed to arise from a state of death we should know that with all that is good must come some bad, how else could we appreciate the good. Remember that the words love defines itself: Life Obstacles Vary Every-day. It is most imperative that we know ourselves if not then find ourselves. If we do not obtain this degree or level of development of self-consciousness, how are we to fully appreciate what it means to be or become an entity of imminence? If we do not have anything within ourselves of any value how are we able to give it to anyone or help guide those of tomorrow towards nirvana. Life is made of diversity, highs, lows, and times of congestion but it are these moments that help to refine us into the warriors sword. Each state that we are in manipulated by the images and thoughts that we have fed our minds. It is in this area that determines just how strong or weak we shall become once we have been tested. "As a man thinkith so shall he be…" "Your condition will not be changed until you change the condition around you." These two statements are two of the most promising yet understated lines in history, all because of their simplicity and completeness. If you do not know who you are and where you are going, then now is the time to find out. However, if you do then now is the time to help someone else.

Complexity or Simplicity

In life one has to learn an enormous amount of things; things that could either help to build upon their future or expedite their demise. Either way one must learn how to maneuver through the obstacles that will most definitely lie ahead. If one is careless and refuses to learn from the circumstances of life then one shall continue to wallow and be succumbed by those very same obstacles that have enslaved them. So why do we become what one should never be- lost. When Moses and the children of Israel were in the wilderness for those 40 years it wasn't because they didn't know where they were going, it was simply because they lacked direction, they lacked faith, they lacked self. So the result was that they could only view the destination and after their allotted time would eventually be able to complete the predestined journey. This is the same endeavor that we must endure today. We lack so much knowledge of our true self that we cannot progress. We must begin to embrace ourselves and begin allowing ourselves to find the preordained purpose of self and the true knowledge that has been placed within. Which brings to mind the question: "What does it mean for someone to be complex and for someone to be simple?" The answer should be the same however, it will appear differently to some. For one to be simple only means that the individual views things as they should. They allow themselves to use all or most of their faculties, they do not wonder through life simply accepting any and everything that's handed to them. They know that they are able to differentiate between what is the complete truth as opposed to what should be viewed as the truth. Now, the complex individuals have a real hard problem grasping almost everything (if not everything). They are the ones that refuse to use any part of their mental power. You could hand them a plate of mess and tell them that its gumbo or what have you and they will just eat it and love it. They view those that are simple as being complex and strange. This is only because they can't comprehend anything or anyone especially things that possess the ability to be viewed in more than one angle. Life is built on more things that possess the ability to be viewed on the surface; it transcends to the depths of the universe. So why shouldn't our mentality do the same? As long as we allow ourselves to be hindered by our own ignorance and stupidity we shall continue to wander in the wilderness of our mind and life. Think of this famous quote- "It could all be so simple, but you'd rather make it hard."- Lauren Hill

Truth

What is truth? Is not truth worth dying for? Answer this, if you had the choice of obtaining freedom from life behind bars or lethal injection by saying you are guilty of a crime you didn't commit would you? Or would you rather die professing the truth until the bitter sweet end? I shall die with honor because I know that it (truth) is worth death. Truth is a hard pill to swallow but it is the best medicine to take, while on the other hand a lie seems to be accepted more yet it's deadly to take. Some would say and believe that ignorance is bliss but in my opinion that's some real BS. If someone was going to draw some blood wouldn't it be better and less painful if it was with a prick of the finger than with a cut across the wrist?? Perhaps people have become too acquainted with lies being intertwined into daily life that it has become almost impossible to accept or acknowledge truth in its purest form. Buddhist say that truth is complete and therefore it's absolute. It is in fact life and what has brought about creation, after all you do believe in The Creator. By whatever name/ title you call it the fact still remains that when you look around you still see truth; i.e. trees, animals, earth, water, sun, stars, etc.- yet we still chose to pollute truth with our own personal lies. We tell lies believing that they make things easier yet they only make matters worse. "I love your dress." "Your breath doesn't stink." "Honey, dinner was great!" Tell the truth it may hurt at first but at least it won't have a person believing something that is completely <u>NOT</u> true. Wouldn't you want to know if your dress is ugly, your breath stunk or you couldn't cook; I know I would that way I don't make a fool of myself later. Suffer a little now or a lot later.

Great Man (Stand)

It takes a great man to do what most have only talked about

To stand up and take on the role without one second of

doubt

To be there through thick and thin regardless of

circumstances

To never turn your back on those that depend or take

cowardly chances

I could only wish to be like this good man one day in this

lifetime

One opportunity to do it again with a new improved mind

Nevertheless there are some great men out there that are

doing what needs to be done

Standing up to daily battles and never bowing out to ever

come

So continue to stand up great man being good and true

Stand proud great man because not everyone can or will do

what you do.

Free

I cannot pretend to be something I am not
I refuse to say that I am cold when I'm really hot
I do not like green eggs and ham
I do not like them, Sam I am
My mind doesn't move to the beat of your drum
My mental capabilities refuse to get stuck on dumb
The world I live in is very complex
The steam off the sun can't compare to what I could vex
Stop, look and listen has been screamed numerous times
How can a corps hear or even read between the lines?
Those that have ears, let them hear
Those that seek knowledge, reject a life of fear
Never does the wind blow on a heart that's dead
Should I really memorize all that I've said?
Why must "I" come before "E" only before "C"?
Why can't the roadrunner ever be caught by Wyle E. Coyote?
Who says that a dumbass could never be the lead?
Just look at '88 and twice his seed
Who in the hell said that slavery was dead
Countries laugh at us when we starve yet they get fed
Impeach that bitch before he brings back the draft
Or put us all on plantations with chains, whips, and well you do
the math
I must stand on my square and follow the night light
Roaming and travelling from the place where the sun shines
bright
Each day I pray to Allah to rescue me
For although I carry chains my mind continues to roam forever
free.

Crazy

Stop the madness! Stop the insanity!

Stop playing with my thoughts, stop bothering me!

It's you that's the problem or is it me

If you are I then whom could it be

Is that a joke are you for real

What's really going on, what's the deal

You're my opponent so I hate you

How do I hate me like I do?

Snap out of it before I snap it in

Eating my lamb flesh inside my own Lion's den

The mind is a terrible thing so it's best when it's tame

This psychological process is real although I don't know

the name

To me I'm just fighting me while loving me yet not

knowing which whom is me

But to you it's simpler than that because to you I'm just

plain ol' crazy.

Inner Being

Peacefully the wind blows through the summer breeze
To and fro it carries words from the rustle of the trees
"Who goes there?" "Tis I the wonderful What; profoundly
known as Who."
"I am the immaculate, indescribable being inside of you."
As the trees cease to blow and the sun begins its blaze of
glory
I am forced to review my life long story
It reads like a soap opera without all the commercial breaks
There was no one yelling out action, cut or take, no
mulligan, rewind, stop or pause
Naw, this is live drama written on hidden clause
Just a print imprinted within each individual actor
No stunt doubles to take our place when fear becomes a
factor
You get one shot for a great performance on this spherical
stage
So break a leg or rather let us pray is the better adage
So let us pray for a proper performance in our attempt at
becoming a star
A star that's blinding to the sight yet seen from afar.

Joker

How could I write and not speak the truth?

I am endowed with knowledge manifesting since my youth

Born into a life that feels uncertain

Killed on a stage with no closed curtain

Marked by society as an inbred menace

More red dots on my face than that little guy Dennis

So why should I care about who I offend?

When so many of you seek death from within

My meticulous ways are shadows in the dark

Spreading heat like a flame thrower coming from a spark

Hate me not but love me so

Through fasting and prayer I increase and grow

Save the applauds cause I don't need your accolade

Patting me on the head like some dog or good house slave

Naw, never that, I'm that field slave that you leave way out
yonder

With shackles and chains, whip marks on my back and
anger that helps me ponder

Calculating ways for my physical to escape because my
mind is already gone

But the physical is not what you desire, it's my mind you
wish to own

So let me bust your bubble for a little moment

How could I give up something when it's all I got; sounds
foolish don't it?

So remember these words as I tell you here and now that
part you could never ever get

I'd rather lose my life 10 times over than to ever let you
have it

Get behind me Satan, step back a second and watch my feet
smoke

You had your chance but I'm laughing now, so tell me
who's really the joke?

Options

Joy and pain
Sunshine and rain
Love and hate
Making love or just another masturbate
Stop or go
Stay at home or go to that show
Black or white
Work all day or party all night
Doing time or time doing you
Live a lie or completely tell the truth
Do wrong or doing what's right
Sit and mildew or get up and bar-b-que
Decide or someone choose for you.

Wise Goat Talk

Who's the wise goat that said "Ignorance is bliss"
Whomever that was must have possessed some of the
dirtiest piss
Why would one want to go through life with closed eyes?
Never viewing the world for who really lies
A life in disguise-
Touched by anger and filled with pain
Killing off any remnant of frustration feign
Knowledge is true power when possessed by capable hands
Although it is free those that seek its enormous spans.

My Thoughts

Slowly, slowly I drift away
Wishing, waiting for another day
My eyes are weak because my mind is lost
My fire is being quenched by the world of frost
Each moment of the hour is stabbing my mind
All of my thoughts are slowly becoming one of a kind
Exodus, release, deliverance, freedom and tranquility
All are one which is taking control of me
I no longer feel myself, although I am new to see
My thoughts escape these walls of insanity
The same old song running with a group of misfits
Misguided people with brain farts that smell like the shits
Domino motha fucka and turn back the TV
Punks wearing tobacco thongs continually disgust me
Bitch this and ho that followed by a nigga please
These are just a few words that degrade and will forever keep
us on our hands and knees
Are we so delirious or just too curious as to our fall within the
structure?
Or perhaps our delusion that's led by confusion of the contrary
conjunction?
Death is reserved so that our souls may be enlightened
While we allow the grip that Satan has on our minds to rapidly
become tightened
"I am a product of my environment", well that's true only to a
certain extent
Production comes from the mind and what you choose to feed it
So until the day or our unpleasant yet evident demise
We must follow the light rather than have the blind to continue
to lead the blind.

Message to the Masses

This is a message to the masses.
To single moms with broken hearts and bus passes
For all those growing up in broken homes without any
guidance
To those kids putting down the toys to gain finances
To all my homies and phonies still locked behind closed
doors
For all those with shattered dreams still lying on pavement
floors
Believe me, I know exactly just how you feel
So know that when I speak, I speak what's real
And what's not I drop like old sweaty laundry
Trying to shake these haters and blasphemers that could
never fade me
The system refuses to allow a young gifted soldier to make
it
So they buss shots constantly seeking to demolish my spirit
Growing knowledge and faith I must wear like a vest
To protect myself from attacks upon the flesh

Pain

What is pain?
Perhaps it's a feeling of loss of gain?
Someone once said it's a must
Even if it cost you someone's trust
Maybe it can help to mend a wound?
How is that when a new one cocoons?
Even the buffoon is able to recognize it
Hell, even he'll never take a plate of decorated shit
Who hasn't seen, it-definitely not me, it loves me too much
Everyone knows it stays next to the sister of such and such
The cousin of my mother's brother
The girlfriend of Joe's lover
Down the street of West Crack Head City
The place that dad goes to find the nitty gritty
Or the new place of work that Ray Ray had the other night
In the club that Bobby went when he lost that fight
Naw, it's the place where Paw Paw once did work
Until that day after 40 years he came home berserk
To those that's in the system it's in the call of mail
It's really nothing at all because even ice water's wanted in
hell.

Who's World is This

Who's world is this anyway?
Not mine to you but who gives a damn what you say
I'm sick of you thinking you actually run this
I'm already 2 seconds from beating one of you nasty
bitches
And a half of a second from bending you over
Sticking a broom so far up your lucky charms till I find that
4 leaf clover
You stink like a wilder beast and that's on a good day
If I hear one more slick comment you will hate you ever
looked my way
You don't want to allow me to be me and you're trying to
stop me from leaving
I tell you what, I'll accept that but how about I stop you
from breathing
Yes I believe in separation and yes I'm full of rage
Yes I am a soldier ready to help you not reach old age
However because of my beliefs and my strong conviction
I'll just shoot you with these lines and a mind of venomous
infliction.

Words

Time has the ability to heal all wounds…
But what about the wounds that refuse to heal?
How shall my soul continue to bear the torture that it feels?
What would make someone do so much harm to someone
that is so close?
More importantly why would someone do it to themselves
even worse?
How long does it take for one to feel secure with this life?
Enough security that a mother not neglect her children or a
husband not beat his wife
One must look within one's self to see the light that shines
within
The realness of self that sticks out like a sharks' fin
Sweet simplicity combined with pure love and devotion
Someone once said that words are more than words
because they express deep emotion.

Words II

When we speak with one another what type of words do we use?

Do we speak words of endearment or words that are profane and abuse?

Why is this so

Do we not know?

Are we too thoughtless to let our true feelings show?

Do words just escape us so we grab hold of whatever may be there?

Think knowledgeable and sincerely if we dare

Our short attention span of acceptance is what we seem to be lacking

We must expand our vocabulary and choose our words carefully so that we're not always attacking

I know that we are capable of doing so because we were created in God's spiritual image

Let us take on the higher plane of thoughtful living rather than the lesser percentage.

Who do You Believe In

Who do you believe in?
Do you believe in life or beginning again?
Do you see the sun as light of the source within?
Is the moon a lamp at night or the point of a new
beginning?
Are the stars just twinkles of His presence sitting?
How about nature and all the beautiful trees?
Are they creating, created or just homes for birds and bees?
What about man and his ability to procreate?
Do you believe in some face, nothing or everything without
needing to definite?
Maybe it's what one believes that drives them on?
To believe not just in self but an indescribable existence
from dawn to dawn
Perhaps you simply believe without question, doubt or
reason?
However you decide to believe just know for this, there is a
season
So continue to seek for the answers to all that's in your
mind
Never define the truth, however you view it, for the truth
could never be defined.

Who Am I

"Who am I?" Is this what you ask?
I am the creation of the Creator blessed with the first task
I am the brother of my siblings and the father of my young
The son of my father and mother of whom the birth song
was sung
I am the follower of the leader and the leader of those that
follow
I am the truth of today and the guiding light of tomorrow
I am the holder of the illumination that comes from within
Possessing a light so bright that it has darkened my skin
I am from the beginning of the beginnings until the end of
ends
I am the roots that hold the tree upright against the
strongest of winds
I am from the "I AM", from Him I simply became to be
From Him came all knowledge so that I may truly know me
I was created by one so I am the one that was given to two
I know who I am so the question now is, "Who are you?"

"What" I Am

Why can't people love me for me?

Instead of just loving what they see

A love that's past physical or mentally

Something that's spiritual and unconditionally

Not for who people say or think I am

Nor for what I can do but for what I am

I am just a spirit living inside this flesh of man

Born into can not's yet professing I can

I am not my hair, my clothes or my speech

Not my walk, address, title or my ability to teach

Not my status, or lack of nor my skin

I am the spirit of God that lies within

A breath blown into clay molded into what you see

Focus your sight past the physical to see the real me

I'm not Kendell, Khalil or someone who's lost direction

I'm just a spirit, God's servant guided by his protection.

War of the Worlds

So who would be foolish enough to throw flames on the
Devil's fire?
Daring him not to drink or take aim on what he desire
It's inane to believe and absurd to conceive that any
opponent that jumps up he would reprieve
Complete fury is all he knows when it's hate that he see
The object of adversity doesn't matter, he doesn't care who
it may be
Don't encroach upon his space nor stare at his domain
You must understand the severity of his double voiced
brain
This devil has a counterpart that keeps him at bay
But when the Angel disappears beware of what's next you
might say
For this beast knows no limits and believe me he has no
bound
So if you fear he is on the loose, get away and get down
Yet this hell is nothing as opposed to when they reside at
the same time
For this war is pure hell as it causes havoc within this
tormented mind.

Through My Cell Door

As I sit and look through my cell door

I think of times past and the guy no more
I reminisce of the stealing, dealing, shootings and banging
The hustles, bustles, hanging and turf claiming
All the days, months and years flown by
Locked up, stepped on days that laugh and nights that cry
Wars, peace, pestilence, genocide and masked destruction
of all kind
The revolution will not be televised because it is a
revolution held in our mind
Hatred, bigotry, adult adolescence or complete stupidity
All of which drives me crazy buy yet we supposedly live in
a complete democracy
Why must our leaders be the worst but the best at being
shallow?
How in the hell can you lead when you never took the time
to learn to follow?
Time is of the essence so quit wasting mine
Lost jobs, pointless war and 4 years of lies
So electing Bush for a second term; I decline.
I guess since this is a democracy I have the right to speak
my mind
However if by chance I begin to speak too loudly I might
be executed as if I committed a crime
Oh I guess Kennedy, Malcolm, Martin and Pac were all just
unpredictable circumstances
Or perhaps you pulled the trigger when you had all you
could stand
Maybe I'm just jumping to conclusions which is something
I really shouldn't do

Or maybe it's the truth which is why all the culprits are still
on the loose
Although arrests have been made on a select few
But why not they were either paid or framed by who else
but you
This is just a few things that I thought of while thinking of
what is and was
I guess when you think of it, he was right… stupid is as
stupid does.

Self-Revelation

Reflection upon one's self is priceless

To be lowered to a station of highness

Take away all possessions and live simplicity

Simply put a life without unnecessary inequity

Material possession have lost their implied meaning

No more blind folds on this man for now he is truly seeing

He sees the more important aspects of life internal and

external complication

Deep contemplation from overdue inspiration that gave

birth to new revelation

For the first time, in what could be a long time,

Every meaning has its own personal line

-Not just a rhyme

So if you would so kindly find

The entrance as I exit this point in time.

The Key Element

It has come to my attention that we as the human race tend to embrace violence and yet we also think of it as profound and inexcusable. How can this be so when it is plainly a contradiction of itself? The reason for this is due to the fact that we refuse to accept the violence in front of our faces, back yard or even the news. However, we condone and are infatuated with the major blockbuster violence that is constantly shown and depicted on T.V. and the cinema. As you can see this is a highly underrated and completely overlooked conflict or our moral, spiritual and ethical character. How can we say that one is bad without pointing the finger at them both, as well as ourselves? The only possible reason for this, that I can seem to find would be that one is reality and the other is fantasy. Yet they both bring about the same result- destruction. If a child grows up watching things such as this on television and being a witness to the same actions in his/her everyday life, then how farfetched is it to believe that child would grow up to carry out those actions; or perhaps to even condone those same actions themselves, having viewed them for so long. Why do parents not look at the money being made from it, that is, actors and actresses making millions for the killing of hundreds of people? Those that are at war are placed in a situation that has only one way to get to the goal. The main focus is to survive so one must consider the options of achieving that goal. One could a) hope that they (the enemy) gives up or hands over what is desired without a struggle, or

b) fight their way out any way possible and realize that it is a win/lose situation. If you win you reach your goal, while if you lose you end up back at ground zero with scars and bruises. So, now you tell me which way has won the most wars? Which one seems to be the only logical way of success? Here is the one fine detail that has been left out of the equation time after time, mind-power (communication). The world as a whole has forgotten about this key element to true survival and national harmony.

Laugh?

Please don't misconstrue my laughter as real joy

Because beneath those smiles could lie tears of momma's

baby boy

But how could one that seems to be so happy feel so much

pain?

Is it due to the fact that he's surrounded by hell's flame?

Being too close to the sun and only getting closer

How hot can it actually get; could it even get

worse-er?

I take that back because yes indeed it surely can

So shut up and be mighty like the renowned superman

I'm only getting older, some wiser but still physically

weary

Laugh clown, laugh until you laugh yourself silly

Hold up! Enough is enough, so quit your laughing at me.

Sean Bell

Rest in peace my Brother and Sister, because Lord knows
you couldn't live in it
Protect and serve who, who the fuck you kiddin'
You're only protectn' your ass as you serve out bullets
Would you please see if we're any real threat before you
smile and pull it?
You know I've been dealn' with you MF'S since I was
about 10
So why in the hell would I seriously believe that the hatred
would end?
Racial profiling ain't nothing but hate covered by a shield
My guess is that it won't stop until we've all been killed
Even if Barak wins tell me what exactly will it prove
When cops still kill and get away and we get no real
coverage by the news
The damage has been done and you still find joy in doing it
You care about the people elsewhere but at home you don't
give a shit
No matter what we have or what we do
In your eyes we will always be just another nigger to you

Oh, you like Oprah because she's rich and generous with her money

But let her not give you some and here comes the names and you actn' funny

Why should we have to fight for rights that's ours since the beginning?

But what's right we fight for and damn sho' worth winning

So excuse me if I'm a little raw because profanity I don't like to use

But damn it you sorry MF's just keep lightn' my fuse.

The Enemy

Prepare yourself for the revolution for it is upon us
It has woven itself into multi-facets and proclaimed to be
just
Still it expands and mingles with us more so than them
We are helping the enemy to over-power us and win
Unity is what's needed for the tables to turn in our favor
We need to begin to reap the benefits of our cold hard labor
Why would we continue to give in and give up all our
energy?
This is nothing new it has been developing throughout the
last century
Look at how we view and treat ourselves so how exactly
are we to be treated
No longer are we being hunted we are simply just being
depleted
"They shooting!" No we are just hanging ourselves with
empty ideas that lead nowhere
The only thing we seem to be united on is that they should
upgrade welfare
"Pass out more stamps and pop out more babies so that I
can get paid."
My God they passed the Emancipation but we still desire to
be enslaved
People please free yourselves, don't allow this cycle to
continually oppress you
Don't get caught up in what's free, get out and work for
those blue suede shoes

It's bad enough we refer to each other with words that attack out mind

Not to mention placing impurities inside our bodies that's designed only to kill off our kind

Who do you think designed the system and society to be the way it is?

The only problem is now we have taken over and began killing our own kids

It's time you begin to stop, look and listen to what's going on

Pick up some knowledge and read about the facts rather than watch soaps or gossip on the phone

Don't worry about the latest trend or what the Jones's are doing

That's not for you anyway its' only to see you ruined

Know who you are, where you've been and where you are going

Know who the real enemy is and the mirror image that's also showing.

Same Old Song

Society is so demented and so obtuse
That even the mere mention of the word should no longer
be in use
Chaos in the home, of the home and over seas
Could bring anyone to live on their knees
Praying to the One that made them
Hoping that one day they can break away from the one that
enslaves'em
Armageddon is drawing near so we must think of where do
we go from here
Although some can't conceive it so they take their lives
because of fear
Mother's crying, kids dying, politicians lying and religious
leaders are molesting more and more
The world keeps turning as hells fire continues burning and
justice isn't blind just a whore
She sells herself to the highest bidder or whoever can
satisfy her needs at that time
Don't worry it won't cost you much just your soul or just
drop a dime
People catching cases and changing faces from cool blue to
envy green
It's not your enemies doing the selling of the telling, only
those from the home team
Just stay focused and deviate away from those that believe
"Life's a bitch then you die"

It's never that but a gift in fact, any other belief is just a lie
Society tells us that it's our youth that fail us but actually
that's not quite true but still bold
For you see the youth and me have learned what we know
from those that are old
However, I beg to differ if we knew that they know we
wouldn't be so damn cold
Misguided by lies about everything under the sky so the
facts need to be told
Society please quit lying to us and entrust us with what's
really going on
Otherwise we continue the lie and the record is never
broken of the same old song.

Civilization

What is this things called "civilization" and to whom does it refer to? Was it some sort of spontaneous combustion of the hidden intellect of the Neanderthals of then and now? Who said that this version of the so called "civilization" was in fact a true revelation or even an actual manifestation of divine intervention? How can a house stand on sand verses a solid base on stone? Even the blocks surrounding the chief corner stone can succumb to the onslaught of poison and or slight maneuvering of its intended direction. If indeed this "civilization" was designed to be the best and the mold of all, why the constant bombardment of conflict and turmoil? Oh I know, "you can't have the bitter without the sweet, because without the bitter the sweet isn't as sweet." That's only to certain degree- the degree of completion- those that have ears, hear; those that do not, shut up and try to listen. In order for one to truly be or become civilized one must allow his/ her mind to produce wisdom; which only comes through knowledge and true understanding. What must one truly understand; perhaps that the complete truth must be and will be revealed as it should also be embraced. History has three (3) sides: yours, mine and the truth. The truth seems to somehow get lost in the middle during the shuffle of life. Which brings us back to civilization, what is the truth about this "civilization"? This is not "The Civilization" nor should it be viewed as such. It is simply a monstrosity of the fabric of development, structure, and the foundation of the human mind. When one creates something one has a specific intention for the creation, whether to help or harm (more so to help than harm). Regardless of which there still is the intention that places the creation in a position of the square, which cannot be escaped due to the purpose that was set before it. Society has concocted an imbalance of what constitutes a civilization or actually being civilized. Why must one conform to an idea that was never designed for him/her? Why set a standard if it is not structured for everyone involved? Why project an image only to dismantle it or obscure it later on? Why even set a caste system that you neither could nor intend to live up to? Perhaps just because we possess the ability to choose regardless of to whom it benefits of harms. Who's to say that this "civilization" is indeed a civilization? Maybe it's just a water droplet in a sea image, it was clear and complete but then it became rippled and deformed....

To Whom it may Concern

Please don't be misled by the lies that society tells you.
Please don't be ashamed to want to search out the truth.
Governments have always been founded on laws that help and hurt.
They help themselves to putting our faces in the dirt.
So many times we have been told that they are here for our protection;
However, I beg to differ for all those rumors are a misconception.
I have never seen a man lie while telling the truth.
The system is built on deception and invalid proof.
Brothers and sisters I beseech thee to not sit back and do nothing.
While politicians and officials take our money and pretend to positively be doing something.
A slap in the face, kick in the back and a punch in the gut;
Combined with a spit to the face but still we must rise up.
Never should we go gentle into that good night and allow our lives to be taken.
My ancestors didn't, so I won't and if you thought different you were mistaken.
Some may be fooled by your smooth speech and honest smile.
Not I, though, well at least not in a while.
Maybe once a long, long time ago;
Never more quoted the Raven and I do too say so.

So my brothers and sisters I pray that you begin to read
between the lines.
Follow your spirit and remember you were born with only
one mind.
It's me against the world; well that's sometimes how I feel.
Then I remember that there are so many out there just like
me that only want what's real.
Let us band together, stand up and fight the good fight.
We must persevere by day and triumph at night.
Pray daily and listen to the One that made you.
Defend yourself with all that you have against those that
wish to enslave you.
I bid you fair well, many blessings and may grace and
mercy forever protect you.
Just know that behind enemy lines and the many lies that
they continuously feed you, just under the surface you will
find what you seek- the Truth.

Your Majesty

I've been fucked more times than a prostitute on a New
York strip
So how could I ever believe I wouldn't make that trip?
To the hospital to get sewed and stitched
Licked and bit by that dog so I guess that makes me its
bitch
Too many times to count in this life I've been screwed over
So now I'm praying for deliverance please save me
Jehovah
You're the King of kings and Lord of lords
Sharpening my mind like a double edged sword
As I walk thru hell's flame right here on Earth
I'm the conceptualization of misery since my bastard birth
So I fantasize of running away to some deserted Island
Sitting in my beach chair watching the waves and smiling
Take a sniff of the aroma, who needs some Caronas
I'd rather sip the nectar from a coconut wearing Roca
pantalones
So I guess now you ask why the aggression and vulgarity in
my rhyme
Fuck you, your majesty; it came in due time!

Upgraded

While you're arguing over the glass and if it's half empty
I'm drinking that water not allowing your weak mind to
tempt me
I'm a natural born hustler better yet an over-achiever
Faith too strong in self and God conquering any disbeliever
Testify
Will I
Can I be
Jett- I me
Watch the sparks fly so heav-i-ly
Soldier talk
Battalion walk
Army of one, one army- war march
Get it done, done got it all mine
In the midst of any storm pitch black I still shine
Never lose always win is my motto
Jackpot king, platinum power richer than the billion dollar
lotto
Went from 24K to 100 proof to sober
Lucky charm flow, golden boy, 4 leaf clover

Hell of a Home

There's no place like home, so there's no place like hell
Although my soul is depleted searching for heaven, yet this
is where I dwell
Engulfed in flaws and quenching my thirst with gas
As a matter a fact give me some ethanol so I'll be health
conscious when I pass
King of the pit since old Lu Lu retired
King turned prisoner since his son was hired
This is one nightmare dream that is way too dog on long
If I'm right I am in the land of the living but yet I feel like
I'm dead wrong
I feel like I'm a shell of a man looking at shells that held
hollow tips leeching onto my vein
Blood thickened my arteries causing tumors and blood clots
in my brain
So just turn off the lights and be easy with all that heat
Give me just a moment to take a breath and for once not be
beat
So again I say there's no place like home, so for me there's
no place like hell
Melodies from heaven rain down on me to cool off the
flames of where I dwell.

Fighting to Win

My life seems like it is trying to swallow me alive

Is my sky still blue or has a purple haze covered my eyes

Glazed over with white pigmentation and stiffen what shall

remain

Tear drops to the ground as they code blue my brain

No more sorrow for the lonely, no more pain for the hurt

Open up the gates of Paradise for me as I George Jefferson

across the dirt

Weezy! Tell Florence to get my coat and she better not be

late

Have Bently to hurry it up because tonight I have an

important date

This time I think I'll drive because this date normally

drives me

Tonight shall be the night that I am certain that I'll be D &

D free

Although I could use a chaser for this date of mine really

begins to show

The last time around I was taken on a ride that I've never

been before

Correction- not the last time but the time before that before that before that

This beast is a mofo, like the Mad Hatter once he has lost his hat

I hope for the best on this experience but I know that if it is like the others I still don't want to go

I sure do hope that this go around I manage to let myself remain like Rango

I'm the law around these parts and my prayer is to not lose that position

In all of my days, I am still wrestling with this beast of a demon condition

Dating a whore of a mind and spontaneous like persona that I feel I may never lose

However, one thing that's for certain is losing is something I refuse to ever choose.

Fallen Star

I believe that one day my life will be more than me
breathing and speaking to deaf ears
Somehow and someday people shall know what it is that
my heart has been trying to say all these years
A voice that screams in the middle of noises and sounds
from every corner of the earth
Harmonizing with creativity and based in a choir that was
predicted way before birth
What actually does happen to a star when it falls from it
position within the universe?
Does it become more than a memory so that it continues to
burn more than something rehearsed?
Why must it fall why could it not just be and help others to
become the same?
Perhaps even greater than what's to be expected so to pass
on an internal eternal flame?
My words, my thoughts, my beliefs are an enigma to some
but the truth to others
They are designed to inspire my sisters, kill the enemy and
motivate my brothers.
So what will happen to the fallen star besides being moved
from its original position?
It shall continue to burn, direct and be directed by the
original source of inspiration.

Smooth Criminal

Why is it a crime for me to be black
To what extent does my complexion require you to attack
Are the written laws written in such a fashion as to be
silently spoken
Must I sell myself short just to please you as a cheap token
Should I deny my heritage and the blood that runs deep
within these very veins
Demonize all that exist and all me that it pertains
You hate my very essence
Seek to annihilate my presence
Persecute my body and enslave my mind
Progressed from Jim Crow to James Crow Esq. over time
Same beast, new sheets
New color, same beast
Just because the howl is different doesn't mean the wolf
won't bite
Chickens are roosting, wolf is on the prowl, so the hunter
comes out at night
Do or die, kill or be killed; no time for the weak to be near
The first shall be last and at last the first must take the last
from here
The time has come to end the suppression
To suppress the degradation
Remove the supremacy that the global minority has used
over the majority
Recognize a leopard by its spots so see the leper by their
complexity
It was us that has made them to be
It is us that continue to not allow the blind to see
Wake up my brother
Wake up my sister

Wake up my father
Wake up my mother
Wake up my land
Quit living on your knees and looking for something to
pour out the hand
The plan was laid out centuries ago
Stop the senseless bickering and let's begin to grow
You know?
Be in it and begin the show
Too much time that has passed and not enough to show for
it
There's too much to lose that worrying about what's already
lost is bull shit
Stop it!
Either we can collectively fight and perhaps die for what
we believe in
Or cover our heads in a nightmare of a dream.

Superstar

So I'm a capitalist because I live to capitalize
On capitalism that America has lived to sensualize
So metaphorically speaking I'm walking on water
The god of this realm so you may call me father
Destruction in your face so a prophecy fulfilled
Revelation of the facts that you wish you'd killed
A testimony to your soul so get up and move
The foundation to the fam so I'm gonna show and prove
Since birth I was blessed with the gift of creation
Speak the word be and watch the words manifestation
I can change water into wine and even reverse the order
An immovable mayhem so beware of the slaughter
Excuse me your honor I need to plead my case
I've been stereo-typed and ridiculed since I stepped in this
place
So if I begin to misbehave then I've stepped outside myself
Perhaps I'll just lose my marbles 'til there's nothing left
So how do I begin to compromise the position I hold?
There's no way I could be a hot boy cuz I'm way too cold
Take out the threat; take away my color so you bleach my
skin
Can't touch this blue diamond so you try my next of kin
We're all protected by the spirit that reigns on high
Don't try your luck just give up or kiss tomorrow good-bye.

Struggle

Alone in a dark room staring at the air of the cold
I sit and ponder of things changing as I grow old

Misery loves company as I am becoming more accustom to
seeing it
Wiping the tears from my eyes as I pick my mind and heart
from hells' pit
The devil and I once were old friends so dear
Although I've tried to part ways, he always seems to
reappear
As a new day begins and another day passes into the night
I think of how tired I have become of always having to
fight
Even though my soul's weary and my mind is drained
I shall continue the struggle that is always a struggle time
and time again.

Savage

So let me get this straight; I'm the savage?

But who was the one that raped and mutilated then drug us

thru the middle passage?

You weren't alone yet you initiated and carried out so

sinister

But this should ease your mind because it was condoned by

a minister

In fact the Pope it was, he so generously gave you his

blessing

Ask him and the other men to look at what they did, is there

remorse in their confession

I know Ol' Willie won't, as you sought him to teach you to

Lynch

Beat one near death and the others will straighten up in a

cinch

So do you still wish to profess that I am a savage?

Ok I'll accept that, which means, I'm different from you

and I think above average

As history has broken you label those you wish to conquer

and destroy

You defile the women and call each man so hatefully boy

This is way beyond civil rights, naw human rights is what it
is
Quit condemning me to die before I'm born…can I live
You've become quite good at killing, stealing, destroying
and anything that profit
Ok, Ok enough is enough "It's that man momma" now will
you stop it
Yet you still manage to muster up the audacity to label
someone else terrorist
When all along you're going down in history as the greatest
ventriloquist.

WE Be Do Boys

Self-determination isn't the strong suit for everyone
But my brothers and I hold carry it like a permitted gun
Perseverance isn't as common as sense should be
Yet my sisters and I walk with it from can't see to can't see
You deny the school we originally came from and force us
to begin again
We not only do it under our own aide but graduate higher
than all of your men
Cum lade, master and PHD you must put beside our very
name
The fact that you hate to admit it means my pride is your
shame
Shame on you for beginning such a hateful trend
Despicable little you for manifesting the weaknesses within
I smell your fear and I see your disdain
I can hear your heart race with anxiety as you try to hide
your shameful pain
Even the playing field so we can see which of us deserves
the lead
Quit cheating by marking the deck and destroying my seed
The seed within our psyche, you planted a virus for
generations to continue to pass on
Listen up and you listen good, your time has indeed come
and gone
The time is now for us to take back what is rightfully ours
Our minds, our bodies, and our inner soul and cosmic
power
Global destruction from you ravenous pigs has been
exposed
It's time to stick a fork in you and burn the body to be
disposed

Reflections of your mistreatment of those that showed you
far too much kindness
You spat in our faces, violated our homes and filled them
with your wickedness
How dare you show such disrespect to those that gave you
life
How dare you smile at us while stabbing us with a knife
Pillage our home, remove from us our everything
Deny us the right to our own space and barely leave us with
anything
Yet you hate us all the more in spite of this all
For after each pitfall you cast upon us, we still stand tall
We are the black and the brown that you wish would just
go away
Each generation you seek to destroy, a new and stronger
one comes in to stay
We've shown you your weaknesses and within them you've
seen your defeat
We are the global majority and it's time for us to retake our
seat.

Question

There's going to be some serious consequences and
repercussions behind what's going on
Motha fucka's pulling drive-by's and leaving stray bullets in
innocent people's homes
Get down! Get down! Is all I hear as shots fly all thru the
house
Swiss cheese is all that's left, not even a punk ass mouse
Death to all those standing not even hitting what was aimed
for
Shots ringing so loudly as someone kicking down the door
Who needs the Klan when we seem to kill our own?
Flag on our face, hat on our head, strapped like WW III,
where did we go wrong?
Oh well, it doesn't matter, "just another nigger dead"
What a huge slap in the face to our race when it's we whom it
was said
Please explain the intention of gang banging when the
intention is never met
But who's to blame when our own neighborhood's a flame
and the nightmares we can never forget
We must begin to think about our actions and whom we
continually hurt
Day after day we are continually placing our own brothers
and sisters beneath the cold hard dirt
Reality check, life is too short to continue to ride in the fast
lane
Stop killing our kind and fooling our mind and begin to place
some real knowledge in the brain
Otherwise, as far as truth lies, we are no better than Cain.

King Holiday

With the recent passing of the King Holiday, I thought it might be most effective to expound on "The Dream". Whatever happened to those dreams and expectations for us as a people and us as a nation? I say people and nation because we continue to be and will be a divided entity, that is until we begin to awaken to that which is reality- The Dream, as oppose to a sleepers dream.

It has been stated before by others however I shall now restate it, there is a reference to us in the Bible (the valley of dry bones) on internally dead individuals (mentally, spiritually and emotionally). We as a people for so long have been lacking in key areas of life; areas that crave attention, yearn for substance and are in dire need for reviving. I'm speaking of areas such as love, knowledge and devotion. We lack love or ourselves because we lack knowledge of ourselves. We lack knowledge because we lack devotion towards ourselves. We lack devotion because we don't love ourselves. It is a continuous circle that will forever repeat so long as we allow the cycle of defective trait passing to be passed through the generations. Some of you may ask "Well how do we do that or who will show us the way?" The way has already been shown to you and the path has been made. The only obstacle that lies ahead of you is you and your mental block. If we as a people would only remove all the lies that have been fed to us by others as well as ourselves we would begin to accept the truth that has always been. We should never have to look towards anyone to save us; we should be willing because we are able to save ourselves. We have all of the necessary tools to achieve a complete rejuvenation if we only began to utilize them. So now what is love and why do we not love ourselves? Love could be described as thought that creates deep compassion and emotion for someone/ something or **L**ife **O**bstacles **V**ary **E**ach day. We can't love ourselves because we don't know how to and more importantly we don't love God. God said since we hate our brother whom we have seen we could never love what we have never seen. Not only do we hate but we despise one another. Just think of how we speak to, treat and mentally abuse one another. When I say one another I am also referring to ourselves as well. Love doesn't curse or use profane language to, it will not lie, steal or cheat. Love isn't here today and gone tomorrow, it is eternal. We lack this love because we lack knowledge of self, knowledge of God. We have never truly become acquainted with self because we are too busy trying to figure someone else out. "Get the speck out of your own eye first."

We are also not devoted to anything that will benefit our spirits and minds not our pockets and eyes. Where things get challenging or appear to be dangerous we give up and run away. Well what if Martin, Malcolm, Sojourner, Harriet, Fredrick, Marcus, Rosa, and so forth would have just said- "Not today I'm tired" or "Not me" or "That's too hard", where would we be? Probably stretched out over some tracks or still hanging from a tree. People we have progressed enough only to see it jump back 20 steps but not by force, simply by choice. We have chosen to accept calling ourselves words that aren't fit for animals. We choose to live in a manner that's conducive to savages. We have chosen death over life.

Today I am beseeching each one of you to rethink and reevaluate your lives. If the life we as a people are living isn't for the betterment of us as a nation, then we must change it and do so quickly. Alhamdulillah (All praise to The God) for allowing me this opportunity to do so.

Food for Thought

What happens when someone gives a misconception of an idea that was actually vital to circumstances that may or may not have manifested? Perhaps lost time and bad blood? How hard is it for people to be completely truthful with everyone, especially themselves? That's not saying that secrets should always be revealed but when seeking a position with someone it should be handled in a prudent manner, so that the outcome can be one that could be construed as the most beneficial. However, when even the minutest portion of information is omitted from the opening statement, the remainder of the testimony could be viewed as a lie or deception, regardless of the fact if that was the intention. What is a weakness? A weakness is anything that hinders one from progression. Most weaknesses derive from old memories which in some form or fashion prevent you from developing into a stronger, more productive and less vulnerable individual. Most individuals don't realize just how deep their wounds extend until they begin to unmask them, simply by allowing themselves to share them with someone. Sometimes we encounter individuals that are in your path to help you to successfully venture the remainder of the path. However, due to our own personal issues we over look them in hopes of someone else coming – but they are not in your direction. You would have found them but due to the neglect of the previous guide we lose direction. Our own expectations of how a person should be (according to the image we desire) should not be another obstacle in the way. We must be willing and wanting to work through our problems in order to advance within ourselves. First we must admit the problem (or that there is one) then we must be willing to deal with the pain that is imminent. No pain no gain!

Prayer

If anyone can help me I am certain that you can
So if you don't mind please listen to the cry from this heart
stricken man
For so long I have been witnessing the abuse of people like
me
Sometimes from others but surprisingly mostly from those
that look like me
Why is this injustice being committed over and over again?
When will we ever realize that the true enemy lies within?
The words we use are so powerful because they are able to
create and destroy anything
Yet we throw around negativity as if it was and is nothing
Perhaps we truly are nothing, for most of us choose to act
out that thought?
How could you ever have begun civilization with people
currently not worth being bought?
Our Kings have become niggaz and our Queens are now
called bitches
Its' a proven fact that our words and actions are what's
depleting our riches
We're robbing our minds and continuously destroying our
wombs
No need to bury the dead, they are living in tombs
They don't even know me but for some reason they act like
they do
Using words to apply to their self-assuming that I am the
same way too

No sir I do not consider myself to be one of the dead
I refuse to live hopelessly blind to reality and continually
be spoon fed
My mind is strong and I grew into these developed teeth of
mine
I don't suck on lies I feed on the truth you put here to help
mankind
So please God if you are willing, will you hear my cry
Please give me the strength to live and help them to live so
that we not just continue to die.

Life

Big Deal

It's no big deal to make you a big deal
Spending my nights dreaming of ways to give you a big
thrill
New components to my master mind of thoughts that play
stop and go with you
Never a sweat broken in the entire scheme of things as this
work is long over due
Break of day I am eager to clock in and hesitant at the close
to clock out
Requesting over time to satisfy your time with work that's
opposite paramount
Sign me up coach for the next play and the one after that as
well
I'll be a one man ironman team for my baby; that you can
run and tell
What's the big deal, she's a big deal to me and to me that's
all that will matter
The record of making a person smile in their heart is a
record that I intend to shatter
Shatter, dismantle, humiliate, shame, or just completely
eradicate
So the big deal is that she's my big deal and making her a
bigger deal is what I contemplate

Forever will

As the day is long and as the night quickly fade
There you and I stand beautifully, brightly shining blinding
the darkest shade
In times gone by and as this time stands still
I love you now, I loved you then and yes tomorrow I still
will
I stand before you a completed incomplete man without
shame or fear to hide
A simple man that only seeks to have you by his side
Take my hand and together let us further begin this journey
in time
In and out of existence, beyond conception of the mind
Space will not be a question nor will there be an incomplete
notion to conceive
The reality that we shall make is one that seems too good
for others to believe
Yet regardless of their inability to possess the ability to
fathom the tranquility of our beautifully woven essence
It is not for the blind to see, the deaf to hear not the
ignorant to bear witness of the divine presence
In and out of space, time will forever cease to exist because
of the time it has stood still
I have loved you then, I love you now and yes my dear
tomorrow I forever will.

Shape up

It's not the shape of your body that defines how I view you; it's the way in which you help shape our relationship that does.

It's not how much time you spend in the mirror or how much you spend on designer clothes that matters to me; but how much time you spend with me and investing in our home that does.

I could care less the manner in which you decide to wear your hair or if you prefer jeans over a dress because it's the manner in which you carry yourself and your womanly mannerisms that matter more.

In essence it's the inner you that exudes and compliments the outer you that in turn captivates every piece of me.

Enemy in me

Sometimes my enemy is my inner me

Clouding my vision to cause me not to see

How shall I be what I am to be?

When all I have is what is hindering me

Let it be

Madness in the mind, confusion in the stride

Wordy thoughts that spit up old pride

Let it be

Voided emotions and overflowing pain

Looking up to the sky for guidance while drowning in the

rain

Neither today nor tomorrow shows any sign of easement

for me

So in turn I guess I'll have to let it be

Pain and Pleasure

If pain is pleasure and pleasure is pain

Then I'm so painfully pleasured that I'm going insane

Laughing so hysterically that my brain is a buzz

So scrambled up in emotions like this is your brain on

drugs

So out of reach yet so close to mind

Too in tune with the Devil but keeping God first in line

I am- so over board that a life raft couldn't save me

Still driving this boat like it was named Ms. Daisy

Captivatingly captive in this distant land

Lost in the transition from my own homeland

Freedom ring loud and clear for us all to hear

Freedom ring so strong and near to remove all fear

Freedom ring so that my brothers can rise and fight

Freedom ring once more for mothers to witness glory in

sight

It's a matter of destiny and a matter of choice

We were born of good nature and as believers we have a

voice

Speak truth, justice and equality things that should be our

God given right

Just like breathing clean, fresh air; it shouldn't from having to fight

No time for walking, I'm swinging on anyone trying to prevent

Prevent me from achieving all that God has meant

So in fact it can't be done for The Plan has to unfold

You can't close this book on me for my story is yet to be told

Another chapter to add, another story to tell

Another day reaching for Heaven and another closer to escaping this Hell.

Winter Rose

A Rose blooms in the winter because the blooms give the
snow meaning
Who would care if the snow was white if the Rose was kept
from seeing?
It's so sweet and simple yet so innocent and complex
It has no concern over which came first or what comes next
A Rose is a Rose and it shall do as a Rose does
It will bloom and give beauty to all that isn't or was
A Rose in the winter gives new meaning to that which is
pure
It brings serenity and melancholy to ideas once being
unsure
To earth the snow shall fall and unto it, it shall demise
Yet a Rose springs up to Heaven and awakens the dreary
winter skies
Who needs another plain white Christmas to know the day
is here
I would rather see this Rose and embrace the love I hold so
very dear
I've seen this Rose for years upon years and how I've
grown to love it so
I shall forever carry this Rose with me even as it is covered
by the cold winter snow.

Beautiful

You are so beautiful, you are the definition
You are just that
You define it because it could never define you
Without you it's just another word
A word with 3 syllables and no real meaning
No purpose
No nothing, just there
But it has you and you own it
So flaunt it, profess your master-hood-ness
This adjective comes alive in your walk
It breaths when you talk
It was created at your birth
And it will live on thru your thoughts
"Hello Beautiful." Is not just a greeting, it's your way of
life
It's how you've made living
So beautifully magnificent
Beautified by your grace
So Be-U-To-The-Fullest Beautiful
Be Beauty Fully made

A Moment

As time moves on and time stands still
I think of past endeavors that I know went against His will
Perhaps time will be gentle and allow me some grace
Bestow me a new opportunity to help save face
A new self, a new life and a new way of thinking
A better spiritual guide to show me all I was missing
The old me has gone away to some other desolate place
Reformation took the lead so that there may be a slow
steady pace
Think about it, visualize it and allow things to just flow
Never get myself in a hurry, give yourself a chance to grow
They say patience is a virtue and that responsibility is a
must
Them both I've learned, and Allah surly knows, so in Him I
trust
To some this may seem corny and a bit juvenile
But this is just a moment a truth that I've been meaning to
express for a while.

Confess

Starting today I shall acknowledge my regression
I admit that I've accumulated too much suppression
Which in turn brought about years of manic depression
So this is my confession…
Confession, confess, but where do I begin
Too much information and lapsed time to go way back then
I will own up to the fact that I am a mess
So why mess with history with a late attempt to confess.

Wanted!

Woman to fill the position of Chief Executive Officer of
domestic and non-domestic relations. She must be loving,
attentive, able to communicate, knowledgeable of worldly
affairs as well as able and willing to convey thus said
knowledge well to others. This position requires dedication,
hard work, patience, maximum energy and effort in minimum
time. There will be long strenuous hours and a prolonged pay
(if any). Must be willing to sacrifice own happiness for that of
others and still manage to radiate and not break a sweat while
doing so. ONLY the strong need to apply because this job is
not for the weak.

Description

A rose by any other name would still smell as sweet
But no other woman on earth could be as delicious as you
my treat
A natural sweetener filled with the purest of honey
The giver of sustenance to which I live, never taking
anything from me
Such a golden brown nectar that enriches my very being
A smooth caress to the touch giving lusciousness a
sensuous meaning
Eye captivating, breath taking so superfluously imagined
and ostentatiously created
Freeze frame appearance races the heart and makes legs
feel weighted
It I could play you in slow motion, it would take days to
complete one frame
If I had my way you and I would be identified by just one
name.

Do You

It's not easy to be you because you carry a heavy load

Sometimes you have to work 10 times as hard just to walk the road

In fact it's 10 times as long as the one normally walked

You're words in action you're not just idle words talked

You're both man of the house and the woman that built it

You give hope to those that even cause to contempt

You're a nurturer so you nurture our center, our mind

When the world turns on you, you still manage a smile that's kind

There isn't a being in this universe more sought after or undervalued than you

Hopefully one day we'll make up and give you yours, but 'til then just continue to do what you do.

Dream Deferred

A dream deferred
A nightmare absurd
A melody of love on lines unheard
A past that's gone and a future that never came
A soul that's lost with no one to blame
I couldn't imagine a day of your life without me in it
Yet I must imagine it thru a window blacked out and tinted
I knew you back then, back before we knew each other
I knew you back then, back when you first knew your
mother
I love you still just as I did long ago
How I wish you were here, how much you will never know
I miss you my precious, you and the good times we could
have had
I think of you often little cherub, thoughts of you joyously
playing keeps me from being exceedingly mad.

Dry Tears

Sometimes I
Want to ball up and cry
As I sit and watch my insides die
Asking the lord why
Must time continue to fly?
Yet there's no peace between she and I
Allahu Akbar, Allah is the greatest
Excuse me my Lord but have you heard the latest
It seems that I am sowing what I once did reap
I'm being eaten alive like grass in a pasture full of sheep
My energy and will are being sucked right out of me
It's beginning to cloud my mind and the vision you once
allowed me to see
That's why-
So in a case like mine, what exactly do I do?
I can't move forward, I'm stuck in love, I'm stuck, so I'm
through
How can a loser ever truly win?
Loveless and childless so where does my life truly begin
Why try, why bother, why even continue to grow?
Why must feces come out in heaps, why I'll never know?
That's why-
I guess since tomorrow is a new day I should try to begin
anew
Being in war is hell but still I try to make it do what it do.

Essence of a Woman

The essence of a woman can make a man's heart melt
It can create emotions that you have never felt
The essence of a woman can surround you with pure
warmth and comfort
It can create excitement like a naval ship sailing back in to
port
The essence of a woman will touch you so smoothly that it
makes you quiver
It will send a rush of passion throughout your body to make
your knees get weak and shiver
The essence of a woman is tough as steel but as delicate as
a rose
The true essence of a woman has the power to open widely
your nose
The essence of a woman is pure and unconditional as a
mother's love
That same essence of a woman is a true blessing that can
only be sent from above
All of these words that I say are true
For you see the essence of a woman, this woman, comes
only from you.

Exertion

I'm sick of this confusion
I'm sick of feeling like using
Being used…
I guess I choose…
To be abused,
So I lose…
So much mental and emotional I exert
That my physical is feeling over-worked
Under paid so I'm overtaxed
Inflation is a mug so how do I relax
This is a recession, the new depression so who's crying
This isn't as good as it get so there's no point in lying
There's so much more to give if you could only see
Maybe the recipient just wasn't meant to be
Quit looking at the past because the future is what's up
What are you waiting for time to run out, really what the
fuck
Seriously it is ticking we only age year after year
Why not be somewhere with somebody instead of saying
damn I wish they were here.

Your Lover

How can I say I love you and not give my all to you?
Words not backed by expression would make them untrue
Words without meaning are just letters placed side by side
Words without direction are just lost without any true guide
They are a part of me to show you how I truly feel
They are a testimony of what's actually real
You and I both know that false agony of defeat is all too
well known
So as I talk the talk and walk the walk as a giant would do
I do it not because I must but because I truly do love you
Not just a love but in it a deepest form
A state of being that places me above the norm
So recognize you lover that's connected to you from within
A rare breed of lovers that' also a dear friend.

Wreck

Just call me Mr. Freeze with this heart growing cold
How silly must I have been for being so foolishly bold?
Playing Russian roulette with my emotions
Pure suicide trying to walk at the bottom of the oceans
So I guess instead of being bitter I was decapitated instead
What I thought was Cupid was the Queen yelling "Off with his head!"
In this Wonderland there isn't any escape from death
Damn it! I knew I should've made that right instead of left
I guess that's what I get for driving with my eyes closed tight
Speed driving equals wrecker and the ambulance to make it a night
Code blue he's a goner unless someone can save him
No use, he quit fighting, notify the corner, the family and them
They say it wasn't the crash that killed him but the attack that followed
A heart attack that is, broken beyond repair, thrown into the pit to be swallowed
Since I haven't a will my estate will be left to crumble
Since I never had a chance to live I won't hear the slightest mumble
All this could have been prevented if I'd buckled up
Or maybe I should've taken Drivers Ed instead of deciding to press my luck.

Words You Speak

Gently, so gentle is the sound of your words on the phone

Do my eyes deceive me or is my heart acting on its own

As you speak to me, it's as if I hear a new tone

Or perhaps new phrases that could only come from a

distant lover

Speak to me, please speak to me more than any other

Your words have touched me like never before

My virgin ears do hear from someone I truly adore

Each moment, every second that passes hits like a fist

Pounding my heart with every beat and never a miss

Be gentle, as you should for anything else is unbecoming of

you

The language that you speak I pray that it's true

Don't deceive me or mistreat me because my heart cannot

take it

The passion that precedes you I hope I'm not mistaken

One too many times I've been done wrong

So the words that you speak I hope isn't the "Same old

song"

Be true to me and I promise I'll be very true to you

No lies beneath my ocean of emotions in the abyss of the

deep, deep blue

A love affair for only a moment is not enough for me

A lifetime of bliss is what I am asking from thee

Or perhaps as long as my ears and heart can stand it

The sound of your voice on this phone is much too candid

Slowly speak to me so that your words and this moment

can last forever

Each word and syllable that you speak to me makes me feel

as though my soul has been delivered

Gently, so gentle is the sound of your words on the phone

Heaven knows where the wind blows but the words that

you speak makes my love flow on and on.

Why Cry

Why should I allow myself to mourn?

Sit and wallow in the tears of a heart that's torn

Feeling self-pity and weak over love that's not

Deciding to leave or rather just turn it's back on me

I stand here begging, pleading please don't let this be

Stay here with me for life not just one night

Equally grounded we'll be together in solace

Deeply rooted we shall stand here in this place

A heavenly kingdom we shall have today and tomorrow

It's ours to have and own not just ours to borrow

If you love me as you say then allow us to be

My lady love please don't take your joy from me

Life is built on love so deep in love my life I wish to share

Loving life with you without regret, without an unwanted

care

'Tis I my love calling out to you from this God forsaken

place

'Tis I my love come out to me, no longer be afraid to show

your face

Allow me the chance to wipe those tears from your heart

with words unspoken softly spoken by this man

As you in turn cleanse my face with the gentle touch of
your hand

Tear eyed and weary I sit knowing I've done all that I could
do

Tear eyed and weary I am although I'm far from being
through

So why should I cry when you love me and I love you

I cry because a wall blocks your heart from mine not
allowing love to connect the two.

Why Me?

Why do I feel so much pain when I should be full of joy?
How is it that someone so full of love be a sad little boy?
Why must I hold back the tears as I count the days until I at
least hear her voice?
How long must I yearn to hear the phone ring to answer
with no choice?
Would someone please lift this world weight off my
shoulders?
Help me to overcome these obstacles the size of mountain
boulders
Help me please my Angel, I need you oh so desperately
I need you now because these tears have now overwhelmed
me
Am I emotional? Yes. Can I help it? I'm afraid no I cannot.
Although she is my Heaven, why must Hell be so lonely
and hot?
No one knows me and sometimes no one actually does care
My Angel does even though she can't always be there
Why me Lord, why must I feel so torn?
I guess it must take place in order for a great leader to be
born
My dearest Angel, my love, my thoughts are always
wishing I were with you
My only comfort is that I'm not alone because what I feel, I
know you feel too.

Wanting and Waiting

Slowly, softly, quietly I stand within the shadows of my
window
Wanting and waiting my love of shortly ago
Where art thou my love, my dear?

Somewhere very far away but not very near
Loneliness and emptiness is how I now feel
A hole that continuously burns within my heart is so very
real
Nevermore quoted the raven as my heart continues to tick
tock to the beat
Drowning and gasping for air my tears and I underneath the
sheet
Praying, wishing and hoping for a brighter day
Wanting and waiting for my love to come take this pain
away
Is she gone from just me or everything that's known?
Oh how I wish I knew where or how she was so I wouldn't
feel so alone
So until my love I hear or see you again
I shall continue to be waiting and wanting you my love, my
companion and dearest friend

Why do I, Do you

Why do I do the things that I do
Is it that I believe that I'm better than you
Or is it more of a curiosity that feels it can't meet its match
Why don't I just abort that child before it can hatch?
Oh how I wish that my sins truly will be forgiven
Perhaps they shall once I change from the life that I'm
living
Am I truly self-destructing or am I just becoming too much
to this worldly life
Imploding on filibusters and conniving busters that are
married to the game like Parkers brothers wife
Too bad for them yet it's too bad for us because we get to
smell the manure that they secret
Bull shit that is like a pasture full of dung that gets thrown
in between the sheets
I'm tired of seeing it and more importantly I'm tired of
having this filth in and around my presence
Perhaps I'll just click my heels, get the hell out of OZ and
tell the Wicked Witch to kiss my ass
Wickedly speaking I feel the need to express myself just as
you did, so open wide and let me pass my gas.

Hello

What is a life without love?
Simply put, a loveless life
A life so empty but made perfect by loneliness and strife
Neglected and un-gregarious is a man without a wife
How inane it is to believe that one could be happy alone
With no one to venerate or love exclusively
No one to love or for them to love me
How pathetic it is for the sun to shine on everyone but me
All I see is cloudy days and more rain for all eternity
Love comes and love goes
Where to, well I guess wherever the wind blows
They say that love, well opportunity knocks at everyone's
door
Not for me though because love don't live here anymore
We've been separated now for a long, long time
I wonder how many times I cross its mind
Oh how I wish at least once throughout the day
If one day it should call a simple hello is all I could say.

Humming Bird

There's no light in this old house of mine

No real meaningful purpose to even look for the sun to

shine

Dark shades of black in a blacked-out room adorn this poor

man's face

Left for dead by the necessity of life snatching away

without a trace

Who will check up on this lonesome son who will even

know if and when I pass?

Lost in the triangle of Bermuda several years ago yet today

still I ask-

"Is there still hope for me? Is there even the slightest

chance?"

I can hear the music playing and I see the crowd moving

still no one will dance

With me or for me because of me perhaps, so I'll just hold

this empty cup in my hand

Water logged and weary eyed viewing vacancies in this

desolate land

Now defined, as resolute, the matter is quickly becoming

Reality check, no not quite yet the song is still humming

It's time for the last dance and still I'm sitting patiently
waiting
Waiting for what, waiting on you, wherever you may be
marinating
DJ here's all that I have, would you please play the longest
song that you can find
If for some reason she still doesn't show, please play it one
more time
She will show, she'll come I know this has to be true
If you must pack up and go, I'll understand and I'll just
hum that long jam until she do.

Hanging On

I...I...I just feel somewhat lost in my thoughts these days
A mind completely submerged in loving you a million different ways
So why is it I can't seem to settle in on just one path to take?
Is it the notion of being inadequate that keeps me awake?
I want to succeed, I want to be great, I want to overachieve
I want to reject failure, to capture your neither-lands, to simply have you believe
There's nothing sexier than to make love to you without a single touch
To be innocently intimate years beyond physical is what I yearn for so much
So tell me do you feel it coming, because I've come just for you
Everything's out in the open with me, so what is there left for me to do
Here I am with my heart in my hands, my thoughts on paper, awaiting your acceptance
Vulnerably dangling on the edge like a cliffhanger on a precipice.

Fighting Days

I may not compose as many lines as I once did but I still
think of you
Every time I close my eyes I still dream of you and all the
things that to me you do
The days aren't as sunny as they were yesterday
Time stands still today yet I feel as though I'm just wasting
away
Today is the tomorrow that yesterday forgot to mention
No more can I expect to see or have you near me
Although you're close by I still miss what was to be
I can't deny the facts that have been laid on the table
All that has been longed for and desired like a child fable
How can a happy ending be near when a piece of the puzzle
just became missing
I looked high and low yet as for its location I'm wishing
I'm doing, you're doing, we're doing what we must do to
achieve success
Yet success without the one you love only brings much
stress
It's today I try to move past yesterday while tomorrow
moves further and further away
So forget tomorrow because yesterday is making it hard to
get past today.

Final Goal

Today I met my destiny
It started directly thru the soul of me
I never could have imagined the immense heat it would
infuse within
An enormous amount of radiant energy, combustion soon
began
Kaboom! With no reservation it soon sounded
Kaboom! Negation of hesitation in unison we compounded
1+1=2 yet these 2 became 1
How can this be so when I was with none?
So shall it be in end as it was so in the beginning
So this beginning begot this, what was once thought to be
the ending
Yet there is an end, an end to what once was
A never ending story of living yet dying from unrequited
love
No need for tears in this story for it has a process that
continues to proceed
Pro-seed indeed come forth with blossoms aside of
fragrance and please hold the weeds
Say it again, say it for me and say it slow as not to combine
Separate the reverence from the re-verse to become sublime
Wait just one minute could this mirage actually be so
Why yes indeed for as so above so is below
Victory is finally here and upon me I can feel the warmth
permeating every faced of my soul
Who would have ever thought that loving and knowing
oneself would make peace the final goal.

Eyes that Tell

You can tell a lot about a person from their eyes
Like how she has a wall built with the mortar of cries
A heart filled with pain a and a spirit drained of energy
Day after day she wonders how could this be
The wonder years of yesterday have come to meet the
gloom of today
Yet it's the hope and sunshine of tomorrow that is clearing
the way
Perhaps he will kiss and caress away the wounds that others
left
Maybe in places that dwell within and not just the outer self
No mistake about it, this venture isn't lightly treaded
Nor will it become overly matted
It's one that not based on soft lips and smooth hips
It's base is much firmer because it was founded on a mutual
friendship
Sure we all have acquaintances and associates
But how many can say for certain that they're worth
growing old with.

Drowning

Sometimes I stare at your picture and as I feel the urge to
cry I begin to pray that this isn't a dream
I pray so earnestly that this is way more than it may seem
Am I wishing too much or is my brain just travelling too far
for me to love, be in love and want it to forever last?
Am I hopeless or just lost in my own translation?
Trapped in my own thoughts of want and a need of an
informal dissertation
Which way is up and how do I get out of this pit
It's hard to get out when all I want to do is dig deeper and
deeper into it
To some I'm crazy for doing so and just wasting my time
I consider it a great investment like giving up a penny to
get back a dime
So I sit here thinking profusely, thinking erratically
thoughts engulfed in waves of you
I embrace my drowning and welcome the sleep that comes
from being lost in not knowing what to do.

My Life

Why do I even try to allow myself to love again?

When I'm only left in the end as I begin

Loving a ghost that doesn't exist

Haunting the past not what is manifest

My life is simple love lost although preferred

The same as Langston with his dream deferred

Although my island is big there's just only me

No love crossing the ocean, no boat to sail this sea

I am the loneliest the number there is

I am the 1 you know even with help from the Wiz

Twenty some odd years with me so that's what'll be

No not us or them no we just lonely old me

It's my curse, it's what my life is, it's my fate

Yes I'm that bastard that people love to hate

No pity, no tears, just nod and kindly look away

To you it would be Black Sunday but for me it's just

another day.

My Son

My son one day you shall know all that really happened

How your daddy caught out and got caught up in

unnecessary gun clapp'en

How he was once real good to your mom until he saw

things for how they actually were

He raised your brother but when your time came he was out

of there

Motives were indeed good and ambition was sincerely

placed

Wrong path was chosen so the time became a mistake of a

waste

My son I have spent seven long years thinking of good

reasons why I made that poor decision

However no matter the excuse it still points to a shameful

reason

The truth is my life was screwed up so much that I didn't

know which way to go

Regardless of what was going on the answer to leaving

should have been "Hell No!"

After all I knew what it felt like to look at life as abandoned

So why after a life of why, why would I leave my first born

up for ransom

The blame is all mine I have learned to accept and admit

that

Praying daily for a chance to take it all back

Please allow me another opportunity to be a father and a

real man

Days in and days out I pleaded with your mother time and

time again

"Fat chance I lost, it's time for someone else to be blessed

by you"

So I shall prepare myself for the day I can be there for you

One day, hopefully soon, you shall become inquisitive of

what became of me

There won't be a need to hunt because over your shoulder I

shall be.

Night Rain

The rain outside could never amass the rain that's in my
heart
Each moment that passes creates a flood when we are apart
"I miss you Babes" is all I can seem to cry
"I miss you too" is what I hear and this is no lie
Never in my life did I think I would feel like this
A pain so powerful that it hurts like the biggest of fist
Dear God please send me some strength to endure and
comfort to sustain
Please give me a rainbow and sunshine rather than this
Noah like rain
Why only when we are apart does it do me this way
Where's the rain when we're together so in together we
must stay
Is this some cruel joke or just a process we must endure
I know there's an answer but what it is I'm not so
"I love you Sweets" I could never say it enough
"I love you too sweetheart", those words give me so much
hope and trust
A hope in tomorrow and trusting that on me she'll be
waiting
With arms wide open and undying love that's never
shaking
So here's a kiss from me to you my love as I tell you
goodnight
Until the time come my Queen when I no longer have
another lonely rainy night.

Night Slumber

Tonight as I lay myself down to sleep
I think of you and I fight not to weep
I reminisce of the days that have past
And I wish for another chance to make them last
When I say that I miss you, you need to know that I mean it
How we conversed and reciprocated one another's wit
Let me just lay here and dream of you and I
Let me awaken to this dream and not to a disappointing
sigh

Peace

To have peace is to be free
To be in a peaceful state I wish was me
Although I have seen joy and more than enough pain
My biggest fear is that I'll never see peace again
My heart tends to beat with big skips
One beat, two beats, stop…whew what a trip
Each day is a new revolutionary war that unfortunately I must
fight
Jump out of bed to gloomy days and climb into fiery nights
I must keep on my vest due to the shots fired by hate
Another day of hell searching for peace as my mate
So little time to look with so much pain
Missing posters posted have turned to an idea found slain.

Name Change

Is a rose by any other name would still smell as sweet
Then how many roses of words would it take to sweep you
off your feet
How about 1 million for each day I want to spend with you
Or even until the sun could evaporate the ocean blue
Never since the world began could words describe how
much I love you
So tell me is it truly my last name you so richly seek
Or perhaps an offspring with rich skin and locks that
enhance her inherited beauty petite
Some may even say my soul is to connect to yours so to
never get lost
Chancing a lifetime of undiscovered happiness or a life of
pain that cost
As I offer myself to you I hope that you in return give you
to me
Otherwise how could love, life, joy, pain, and the name
change ever be?

No Apologies

Why should I apologize for saying what's true
Why should I say I'm sorry for expressing my love to you?
Of so I'm late, ok so maybe I'm attempting to make
amends
Ok so what that I do and honestly and truly love you my
lover and friend
Yes I hate the way I was and yes I am as you see
Yes I do sincerely believe that this is mean to be
Because if it wasn't why would your love have control of
me...
Excuse me, no forget that I mean what I said
If loving you is wrong, then I'm wrongfully dead
I do hate the time we lost but still we have so much time to
gain
I'm willing to sacrifice myself for you, because your love
heals all my pain
All my misery, discomfort, downs and lonely drops of tears
Our hearts beating as one strengthens me enough to
diminish all my fears
So if loving you too much is the shameful act that I'm
guilty of
Then guilty I'll be but not being apologetic of giving you
all my love.

Passion

Shh… Don't speak
Just lay here beside me until I fall asleep
No sex, no kisses just your body beside mine
Let the moment speak for itself and mature like wine
Lost in time
Lost in the moment yet trapped in my thoughts
Comfort me once more, be my consort
Now tell me your thoughts but utter not a word
Let your heart speak to me without being interred
Your skin being as soft as a smile in the morn
Keep me within you don't let me go away torn
I can't shake you from my mind even though I feel I should
I must focus on certain tasks but exactly how I could
Wait, wait a minute, what am I doing here
I can't give you this power part of me its caution not fear
Too much power you may have which puts you in control
of me
I', a free spirit a free man so a slave I can't be
But yet I'm snatched away by emotions that twist and turn
I'm by myself or do you too yearn
For passion of the highest degree somewhere around ever
Or am I just dreaming of a desire that's only never.

Past, Present, Future

To what do I owe this foolishness which surrounds me?
Perhaps it was invited by the foolish behavior that was
brought by he?
Neither I, he nor thee shall surpass she
However all must be removed far away from me
My past must never meet my present
However the past must never be considered irrelevant
Both are the truth, both are a part of me
How true that may be but neither shall hinder me
Lost love, youthful lust, adolescent pride, bombarded by
teenage hormones
All are equally potent in the molding, framing and
mechanics of all youths-
…But I digress…
A life not lived is not a life at all
So my past must not be allowed to determine my all
My present must be maximized in the moment
So my future will be the greatest… won't it?

Not Again

Once again it seems as though my heart leapt before my mind

Once again it seems as though love may have failed me yet another time

I do so hope that it hasn't and that it is only evil suggestions

If I could only speak with you to get answers to my many questions

Where have you been this past long week?

Where have your lips been and those words you softly speak?

What has been going on with my dearest sweets?

What is the meaning of this travesty for us not to meet?

Ok only once within five long days and 21 before

Please I beg of you don't tell me that you don't love me anymore

I'm sure we can work this out but if you must go then so be it

Only tell me now and bury my heart rather than just keep it

It's no secret about my love, the world knows how I feel

They speak of you how I think of us as a lifelong deal

I seek refuge in the Lord of mankind because this is what's
written

Cupid struck me with his arrow and to you I am truly
smitten

She loves me, she loves me not, she loves me, she loves
me...

Not only can I not think of it but you without me I can't see

I'm overcome by all types of emotions the man being
chagrin

Please Lord don't let me live out those words, you know
the ones- Not again!

Pleasurable Pain

As cries fill the long dreary nights
Days come with stares and mental fights
What is to become of tomorrow or even today?
What will make her go from whence she stay?
My heart beats with agony from seconds of pleasure
Can you stand the rain or better yet can I stand the weather?
Tried and tested yes I know we shall all be
Stand firm and secure in all I do and don't see
As love leaves one house it builds a home
One built on future dreams, past let downs and a today on
it's on
How could one so happy feel so alone and confined?
Placed in a box with nothing that does surround
Push pause and rewind this track to the intro
Bump that funky beat to make my heart flow
Tell misery that love lives here and it's got to go
My Angel helps me with the battle so Devil hell no
We are riding for the long haul until the very end
My Angel and me and the royal lineage that lies within.

Pressure

It's funny, they say be careful what you wish for because
you just might get it
Well I got what I wished for and even got to feel pathetic
Un-copacetic
Forget it
I was willing to accept the pain she carried and I believe
that's what I got
I just didn't know it would carry me past boiling hot
Nonstop
Why not
So you ask can I handle the pressure that I have
If I couldn't I wouldn't so you do the math.

Prayer (Thank You)

Thank you God for smiling down on me
Blessing me with a woman, a daughter, and a child to be
Never did I imagine such wealth being bestowed upon a
wretch like I
Never did I think I could ever taste a slice of Heaven's pie
Dear God make me strong, strong enough to handle such
joy
Guide my steps and mind as I help raise a beautiful girl and
possibly a baby boy
Keep my heart pure so that I not neglect or disappoint my
partner to be
Please help me to truly be for them all that you created me
to be
Show me my faults and current them as they may come
Endow me with enough wisdom to flourish this family and
our kingdom
I know that my faith in you is strong enough to just hold
and maintain
That's why I know you shall continue to bless us to never
lose, only to gain.

Prayer for Strength

Allah I pray that she keeps me in her heart and mind
That she knows that when looking for love it's me she find
I love her so, I pray that she loves me the same
Hoping that I can say Mashallah to her accepting my name
Although it feels like I'm giving up so much to gain so
much more
The basic truth is that it's a small item in this heavenly
store
We all know that I am just a mere human so I still have a
base desire
But we also know that you are the supplier of needs and
that you never tire
It's been two complete days and I'm wondering just how
many more to go
Could it be just one or are there truly 5 more to show
There isn't any other that I want nor was there any other
created specifically for me
So for your pleasure Allah I shall continue to be strong for
she.

Rejoice in Crying

If I die tonight, tomorrow would you cry for me?
Please don't; my request is just rejoice in knowing me
So today be sure to do all that you could possibly do
No regrets, no second chances, make this one time
completely true
If it is something you wish to say please speak it now in
this moment
What's the purpose of roses for the dead; that makes sense
don't it?
Not to say I plan on leaving you soon any time
But who's to say that the day isn't hurting for this old heart
of mine
So if you love me then hold on to me as tight as you can
Don't neglect our connection nor deny yourself this good
man
To say that you can't is shortening your ability to do so
Don't cut yourself short from going for what you know
You know you want me so take hold of what you want
Stand tall and claim your prize, don't be afraid to flaunt
People only cry at funerals because they wish they had or
wanted more of what's past
How about instead we create memories that will last and
last.

Standing Time

As time stands still and the world continues to turn, my
whole perspective of life begins to reform

I must reevaluate the former self by transforming my
present self from the norm
Change my view points as well as my stand points
Practice empowerment and righteous development, rather
than silly and sinister will and won'ts
Take time to smell the roses and sway with the trees
Listen to the song of the birds and the honey bees
Take the scenic route home with my love
Lay under the moonlight and stare at the stars above
Exhale passion throughout my body with each tender
breath
Slowly and tenderly with every motion each I give myself
Not just one night but for all of my life
With long beats of my heart she becomes my soul wife
My angel, my prize, my gift of pleasure
A fulfillment of erotica that surpass any measure
I give her my all and an "I do" sealed with a kiss.

Dream

To dream of a blue sky over a blue ocean
Or perhaps an island of beautiful women and a gallon of
love potion
To think of all days well spent
Or a life full of joy without any corporal punishment
To wake up each day to warm days and warm nights
To see a smile each day from the love of your life
To say "Baby I love you" and know that you meant it
To be surrounded by true love ones not those that make you
feel like shit
To take a long walk on the beach with the moon as your
light
To not come to an empty home night after night
To feel pure comfort and warmth in the arms of my baby
To not be with someone that is constantly driving you crazy
To overflow with an infinite amount of wealth
Not financially but emotional, spiritual, physical and
mental health
When I dream I refuse to dream in black and white
For you see I always dream as colorful as rainbow sun light
I could go on forever describing what I dream when I do
But the fact will forever more be that I dream about you!

Dream II

Is it so wrong for me to dream of having an "I do kiss"?
Or is this a midsummer night dream that I should just dismiss?
How could I simply displace a dream that fill my deepest thought?
It's not just a want it's a need to fulfill all that I've been taught
But the one I want doesn't seem to believe as I do
So I guess it will come a time when I'll have to accept someone new
This is neither something I want nor a moment I wish to see
Regardless of which, the option of settling just isn't for me
So I dream, as Maya still rises
So I dream, as I drown in her eyes
I drift on the thought of her with me
And what we could share
So as I lay me down to sleep and dream, oh please be there.

Dream III

It pains me to imagine you and I not being together
So it's killing me to think of having to see another
This is wrong, so why must it be
Why must the dream of life only come to me?
I'm not for playing games I can only be serious
So for me to love another is what's called delirious
Yet I'm curious…
Is this just a temporary no or did someone use a chisel and
stone
Will I be united with her or must I live alone
One day there may come a time when I'll have to accept
her view
When and if that day does come the question will be "so
now what do I do?"
Do I wallow in despair or do I shake it off and move on
Move on! Move on to what?! My baby, my heart is gone
So maybe you can't always get what you want, true indeed
But I know that for sure I will get what I need.

Bleeding Heart

As you read these lines watch how my heart bleeds in the
many shades of blue
Closely listen to my heart sing these unspoken words to
you
Tell me how can I be found yet still feel somewhat lost
No matter how much I want happiness I can't get it without
knowing the cost
I give and give so that I may get but I feel it being slowly
taken away
So as I give it liberally and so deliberately I'm my own
enemy some would say
It is I that stands in front of me being as happy as I could
possibly be
No one else is to blame for my short comings just pitiful ol'
me
If I fall it's because that's what I chose to do
If I fall it may be because that's what I'm use to
So I shall rise above my former self to a plateau that sits
above the skies
Look deeply to see a soul without fear, look deep within
these eyes
I only fear being inadequate for you and others I truly love
Search beyond this flesh to find the purity like the whitest
of white dove

Absence

Who in the hell said absence makes the heart grow fonder?

Who had the audacity to lie like that I wonder?

Seriously who would say such a thing without knowing
how it feels

Take it from me people, a distant lover can kill

Two hearts shouldn't be apart for too long

For one will stray or both will go wrong

You know, not quite right, as hearts should go

Here today, gone tomorrow but come back- don't know

Maybe if it's old love but not one being refreshed

Because what appears today, tomorrow may be vanquished

So cheers to you for surviving thru the storm

But believe you me that's far from the norm.

Clear My Throat

Um hum, excuse me as I clear my throat so that I may get
these words off my chest
This is what some would call a manifesto of emotions that I
have to manifest
Although I am living in hell and can't seem to see what
anything is really worth
Each time I bask in your angelic glow I am reminded that
"I got Heaven right here on Earth"
You have no idea the amount of restoration your being has
bestowed upon me
Ahh, let me stop and smell these roses because Suger you
really got me
As a matter a fact, let the truth be known I prayed for you
The only reason I asked God to come here, and put up with
this bull, was to find you
I could have went other places but I knew it was something
out here just for me to see
Thank God Almighty for saving such a special Angel just
for me
When I'm with you I adore you and when I'm away I do so
miss that feeling
Tick toc down the seconds to be with my last oohh umm
you know healing
So umm excuse me Miss as I clear my throat so that I may
get these words off my chest
Wait, wait, wait it's too soon, too soon so the rest- for now
I will just suppress.

Enchanted

How dare you be so enchanting?
Gasping for my breath I how you have me
Struggling just for a moment of air, so breathe life into me
You leave so does my wind, you're my source of life; don't
you see
Can you say captivating?
Or perhaps titillating?
There's no denying it I'm hooked, I'm hooked on you
Watch me move to the sound and motion of your flute
I've never felt like this before
Thoughts of someone, loving someone, neither nor
It's a complete embodiment of adore and towards you it's
directed
Mesmerized by you, a gift for me you were selected
A union to be perfected
Never to be neglected
I'm lost in translation, enchanted by your feminine mojo
swaying with those Baby Phat hips
Hypnotized by those honey brown eyes and those
lusciously full lips.

What Would it be like?

What would it be like?
If I were to fall in love with you and you with me
What would it be like?
If I could kiss you whenever and wherever we wish to be?
Would it be heavenly or divine as some would say?
Or would it be exciting and playful all the day
Could you possibly have the courage to express your
feelings for me?
Or would that be too much to ask from thee?
I have a notion that you are ready for love, ready for me
I only wish that this isn't just a personal fallacy
How could I expect you to wait for me to step away from
what is expected?
How could I expect you to walk away from a place you
protected?
Hindered and suffocated by those that only mean you well
I too want what's best for you even if causes me pure
Hell
My deepest desire is for you to happy, healthy and free
Even at the cost of my happiness of you being with me
So my dear, my love, & my source of a heart that is good
I wanted you to have this thought of mine of what possibly
could.

Vocabulary

Allahu Akbar- The God is greater (than anything imaginable)

Alhumdullilah- (All praise to the God)

Masha Allah- (The God has willed it

Aoodu Billihi Minash Shatan-ir Rajeem-

(I seek refuge with The God from the rejected accursed one)

www.ingramcontent.com/pod-product-compliance
Lightning Source LLC
Chambersburg PA
CBHW060258050426
42448CB00009B/1681